I0426200

Assessment of Coastal Water Quality at Timucuan Ecological and Historic Preserve, 2008

Natural Resource Report NPS/SECN/NRR—2009/108

Joe DeVivo
National Park Service
Southeast Coast Inventory and Monitoring Network
100 Alabama St., SW
Atlanta, GA 30303

Phillip H. Flournoy
University of Georgia
Marine Extension Service
0101 Fisheries Building
Brunswick, GA 31523

Katy Austin Smith
University of Georgia
Marine Extension Service
715 Bay Street
Brunswick, GA 31520

May 2009

U.S. Department of the Interior
National Park Service
Natural Resource Program Center
Fort Collins, Colorado

The Natural Resource Publication series addresses natural resource topics that are of interest and applicability to a broad readership in the National Park Service and to others in the management of natural resources, including the scientific community, the public, and the NPS conservation and environmental constituencies. Manuscripts are peer-reviewed to ensure that the information is scientifically credible, technically accurate, appropriately written for the intended audience, and is designed and published in a professional manner.

Natural Resource Reports are the designated medium for disseminating high priority, current natural resource management information with managerial application. The series targets a general, diverse audience, and may contain NPS policy considerations or address sensitive issues of management applicability. Examples of the diverse array of reports published in this series include vital signs monitoring plans; monitoring protocols; "how to" resource management papers; proceedings of resource management workshops or conferences; annual reports of resource programs or divisions of the Natural Resource Program Center; resource action plans; fact sheets; and regularly-published newsletters.

Views, statements, findings, conclusions, recommendations and data in this report are solely those of the author(s) and do not necessarily reflect views and policies of the U.S. Department of the Interior, NPS. Mention of trade names or commercial products does not constitute endorsement or recommendation for use by the National Park Service.

This report is available from the Southeast Coast Network and the Natural Resource Publications Management website (http://www.nature.nps.gov/publications/NRPM).

Please cite this publication as:

DeVivo, J. C., P. H. Flournoy, and K. A. Smith. 2009. Assessment of coastal water quality at Timucuan Ecological and Historic Preserve. Natural Resource Report NPS/SECN/NRR—2009/108. National Park Service, Fort Collins, Colorado.

NPS 100008, May 2009

Contents

Summary and Key Findings

1. In July, 2008, the Southeast Coast Network and the University of Georgia conducted an assessment of water and sediment quality at Timucuan Ecological and Historic Preserve as a part of the NPS Vital Signs Monitoring Program.

2. Monitoring was conducted following the methods developed by the Environmental Protection Agency as a part of the National Coastal Assessment Program (EPA 2001).

3. Water quality at TIMU was determined to be *Fair*. This rating was determined based on the fact that more than 50% of the sites sampled were in either *Fair* or *Poor* condition (Figure 1).

4. Sediment quality at TIMU was determined to be *Good*. This rating was determined based on the fact that less than 5% of the sites sampled were in *Poor* condition, and less than 50% of sites were in combined *Poor* and *Fair* condition (Figure 2).

5. Concentrations of Total Dissolved Phosphorus, Chlorophyl a, and Total Organic Carbon most frequently caused sites to rank as *Poor*.

6. Although Dissolved Oxygen levels ranked *Fair* at six sites, none of the readings were below State water quality standards.

7. Sediment contaminants were not a determining factor in overall sediment quality (all sites rated *Good*).

8. Sites ranked most frequently as *Poor* were concentrated in the headwaters of the Nassau River.

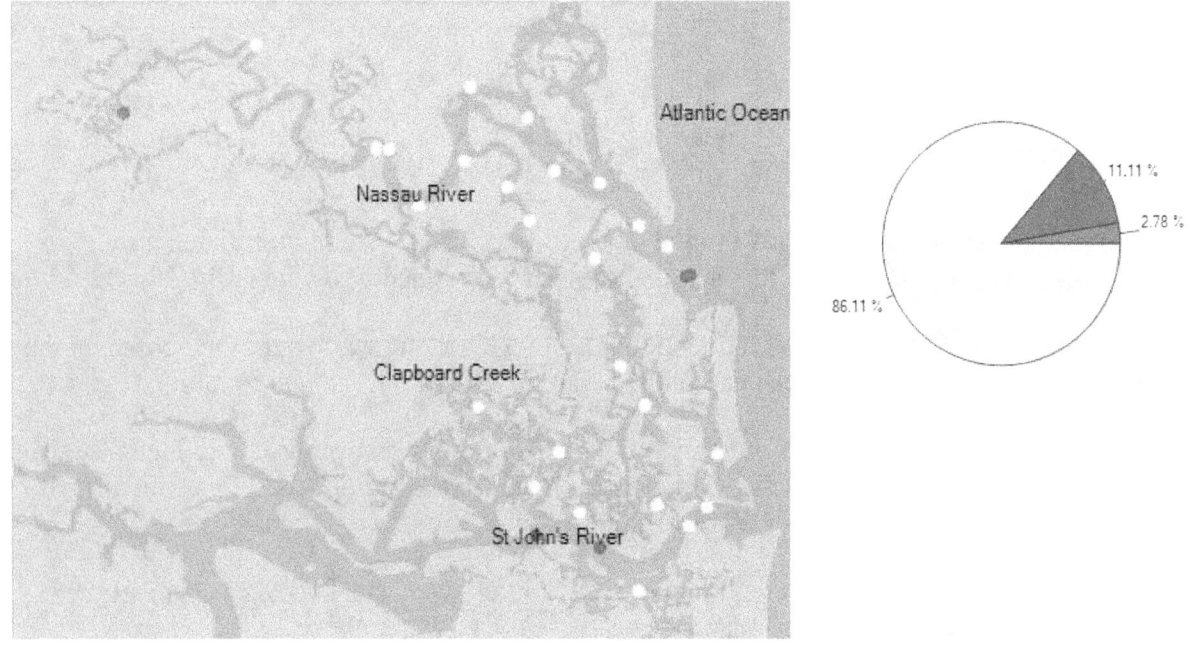

Figure 1. Assessment of Water Quality Index scores at Timucuan Ecological and Historic Preserve, 2008, and percentage of sites in each condition category. Sites denoted as green received a *Good* rating, yellow sites ranked *Fair*, and red sites ranked *Poor*.

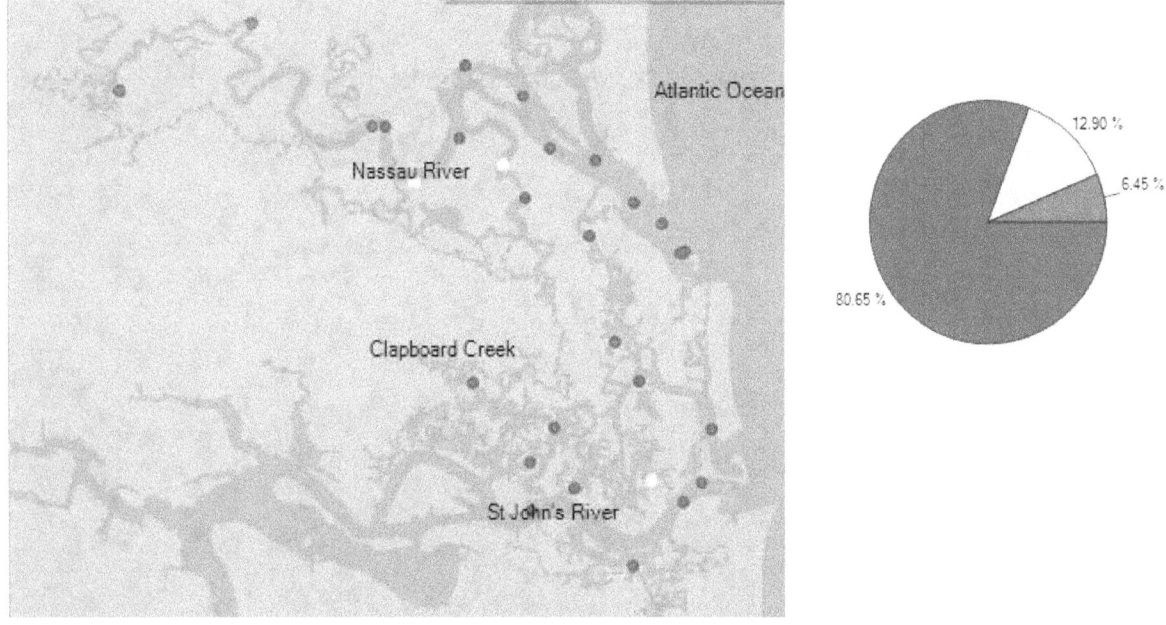

Figure 2. Assessment of Sediment Quality Index scores at Timucuan Ecological and Historic Preserve, 2008, and percentage of sites in each condition category. Sites denoted as green received a *Good* rating, yellow sites ranked *Fair*, and red sites ranked *Poor*.

Introduction and Methods

In July 2008, the Southeast Coast Network and the University of Georgia conducted an assessment of water and sediment quality at Timucuan Ecological and Historic Preserve (TIMU) as a part of the Network's Vital Signs Monitoring program (DeVivo et al., 2009). The monitoring was conducted in estuarine and tidal creek waters following the methods developed by the Environmental Protection Agency's National Coastal Assessment Program (U.S. EPA 2001). Descriptions of the water quality parameters and the assessment criteria are from EPA's National Coastal Assessment II Report (2005).

Estuaries are semi-enclosed coastal bodies of water that have free connection with the open sea and within which sea water mixes with fresh water. The key feature of an estuary is that it is an interface between sea water and fresh water and there is an influence of the ocean tide creating a dynamic relationship between the two waters. Estuaries contain critical habitat for a variety of fish and wildlife species. They serve as nursery habitats for fish, crustaceans, and shellfish and foraging habitat for birds and mammals while providing a multitude of recreational opportunities including boating, fishing, and bird watching. These are fragile ecosystems vulnerable to impacts caused by development and use. Severe impacts including alterations to hydrodynamic processes, exposure to levels of chemical contaminants that cause mortality, altered growth, and reduced reproduction and exposure to more frequent and severe hypoxia can be seen in estuarine habitats from urban and industrial development (Lerberg et al. 2000). In addition, macrobenthic communities in impacted areas are characterized by low diversity, low numbers of rare and pollution sensitive species, and low macrobenthic abundances (Lerberg et al. 2000). In areas with increased impervious cover, stormwater runoff is flashy and greater then natural amounts of fresh and polluted waters are released into estuaries (Holland et al. 2004).

Water Quality

The water quality index is made up of five indicators: nitrogen, phosphorus, chlorophyll *a*, water clarity, and dissolved oxygen. Some nutrient inputs to coastal waters (such as nitrogen and phosphorus) are necessary for a healthy, functioning estuarine ecosystem. When nutrients from various sources, such as sewage and fertilizers, are introduced into an estuary, the concentration of available nutrients will increase beyond natural background levels. This increase in the rate of supply of organic matter is called eutrophication, which may result in a host of undesirable water quality conditions. Excess nutrients can lead to excess plant production, and thus, to increased chlorophyll, which can decrease water clarity and lower concentrations of dissolved oxygen.

The water quality index used in this report is intended to characterize acutely degraded water quality conditions. It does not consistently identify sites experiencing occasional or infrequent hypoxia, nutrient enrichment, or decreased water clarity. As a result, a rating of poor for the water quality index means that the site is likely to have consistently poor condition during the monitoring period. If a site is designated as fair or good, the site did not experience poor condition on the date sampled, but could be characterized by poor condition for short time periods. In order to assess the level of variability in the index at a specific site, increased or supplemental sampling is needed.

Sediments

Another issue of major environmental concern in estuaries is the contamination of sediments with toxic chemicals. A wide variety of metals and organic substances, such as polycyclic aromatic hydrocarbons (PAHs), polychlorinated biphenyls (PCBs), and pesticides, are discharged into estuaries from urban, agricultural, and industrial sources in the watershed. The contaminants adsorb onto suspended particles and eventually accumulate in depositional basins where they can disrupt the benthic community of invertebrates, shellfish, and crustaceans that live in or on the sediments. To the extent that the contaminants become concentrated in the organisms, they pose a risk to organisms throughout the food web—including humans.

Several factors influence the extent and severity of contamination. Fine-grained, organic-rich sediments are likely to become resuspended and transported to distant locations and are also efficient at scavenging pollutants. Thus, silty sediments high in total organic carbon (TOC) are potential sources of contamination. Conversely, organic-rich particles bind some toxicants so strongly that the threat to organisms can be greatly reduced.

The physical and chemical characteristics of surface sediments are the result of interacting forces that control chemical input and particle dynamics at any particular site. In assessing coastal condition, researchers measure the potential for sediments to affect bottom-dwelling organisms. The sediment quality index used by the SECN is based on two indicators of sediment condition: sediment contaminants, and the sediment TOC concentration.

Sample Locations

Timucuan Ecological and Historic Preserve is situated entirely within Duval County and the city limits of Jacksonville, FL, and encompasses approximately 46,000 acres between the St. Johns and Nassau rivers. The southern third of the preserve lies at the mouth of the extensive St. Johns River watershed, which includes parts of Duval and several other counties for approximately 300 miles to the south. The St. Johns River is heavily impacted by agricultural, industrial and urban pollution; however, marine tidal waters near its mouth serve to ameliorate pollution through dilution and flushing. The northern two thirds of the preserve lie within the Nassau River drainage basin, a small watershed that covers parts of Duval and Nassau counties. The Nassau River watershed has not yet experienced the concentrated urban and industrial growth found along the St. Johns River; still, portions of the watershed exhibit poor water quality. The area surrounding the preserve to the west and north is predominantly marsh and low uplands utilized for timbering, residential and agricultural uses.

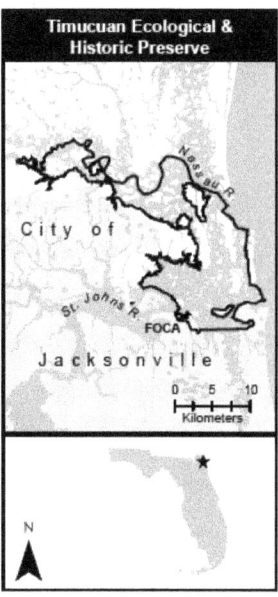

Thirty sites within the boundaries of TIMU were randomly selected following using methods developed by the U.S. EPA (Stevens 1997; Stevens and Olsen 1999; Stevens, D. and A.R. Olsen 2004) (Figure 3).

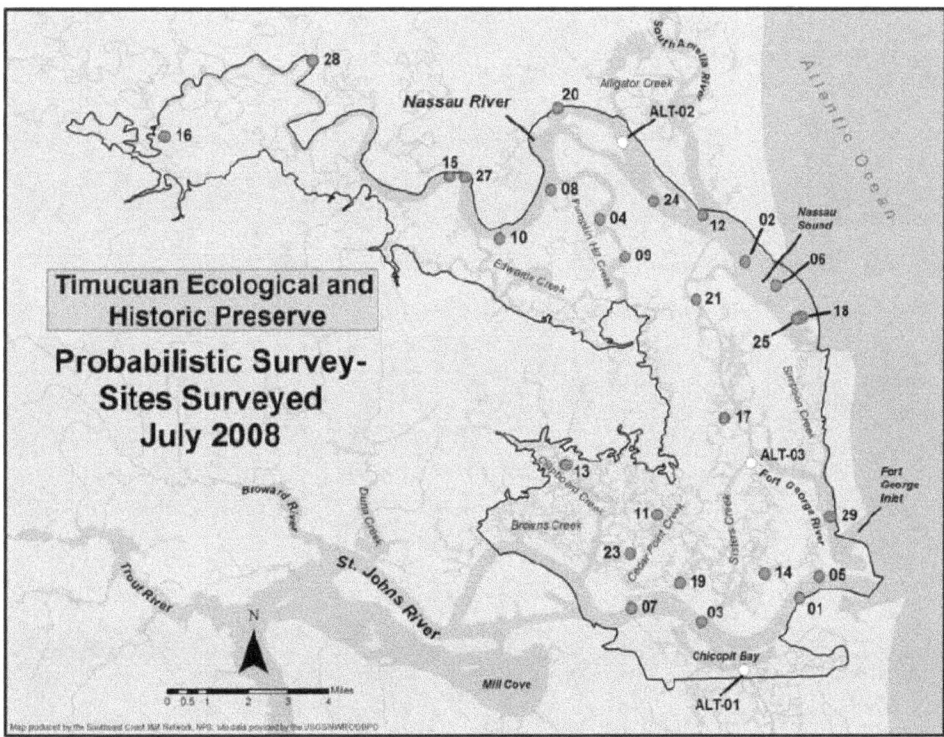

Figure 3. Sites surveyed during 2008 assessment of coastal waters (red dots). Yellow dots indicate alternate sampling sites also monitored as a part of the assessment.

Assessment Criteria

Water Chemistry Assessment

Water quality was assessed for each of the parameters following the East / Gulf Coast site criteria in EPA's National Coastal Assessment II Report (2005) (Table 1).

Table 1.
Condition criteria for water quality parameters collected by the Southeast Coast Network during Coastal Water Quality monitoring.

Rating	Water Clarity Index (WCI)	Chlorophyl a (ug/L)	Total Dissolved Nitrogen (mg/L)	Total Dissolved Phosphorus (mg/L)	Dissolved Oxygen (mg/L)
Good	<2.3	< 5	< 0.1	< 0.01	> 5
Fair	2.3 – 2.99	5 – 20	0.1 – 0.5	0.01 – 0.05	2 – 5
Poor	> 3.00	> 20	> 0.5	> 0.05	< 2

After total dissolved nitrogen (TDN), total dissolved phosphorus (TDP), chlorophyll a, water clarity, and dissolved oxygen were assessed for a given site, the water quality index rating was calculated for the site based on these five indicators. The index was rated good, fair, or poor using the criteria shown in Table 2. Criteria for determining park-wide assessments are also presented in Table 2.

Table 2.
Condition criteria for summary water quality assessments by site and by park.

Rating	Site Water Quality Index Rating	Park Water Quality Index Rating
Good	A maximum of one indicator is fair, and no indicators are poor.	Less than 10% of sites are in poor condition and less than 50% of sites are in combined poor and fair condition.
Fair	One of the indicators is rated poor, or two or more indicators are rated fair.	10% to 20% of sites are in poor condition, or more than 50% of sites are in combined fair and poor condition
Poor	Two or more of the five indicators are rated poor.	More than 20% of sites are in poor condition
Missing	Two components of the indicator are missing and the available indicators do not suggest a fair or poor rating	

Sediment Chemistry Assessment

There are no absolute chemical concentrations that correspond to sediment toxicity, but Effects Range Low (ERL) and Effects Range Median (ERM) values are used as guidelines in assessing sediment contamination (Table 3; Long et al., 1995). ERM is the median concentration of a contaminant observed to have adverse biological effects in the literature studies examined. A more protective indicator of contaminant concentration is the ERL criteria, which is the 10th percentile concentration of a contaminant represented by studies demonstrating adverse biological effects in the literature. Ecological effects are not likely to occur at contaminant concentrations below the ERL criterion. The criteria for rating sediment contaminants at individual sampling sites are shown in Table 4.

Table 3.
Sediment Contaminant guidance values. ERL (Effects Range Low) thresholds are determined for each chemical as the 10th percentile in a database of ascending concentrations associated with biological effects. ERM (Effects Range Median) thresholds are determined for each chemical as the 50th percentile (median) in a database of ascending concentrations associated with adverse biological effects. From Long et al. (1995).

Contaminant	ERL	ERM
Metals[a]		
Arsenic	8.2	70
Cadmium	1.2	9.6
Chromium	81	370
Copper	37	270
Lead	46.7	218
Mercury	0.15	0.71
Nickel	20.9	51.6
Silver	1	3.7
Zinc	150	410
Organics[b]		
Acenaphthene	16	500
Acenapthylene	44	640
Anthracene	85.3	1,100
Flourene	19	540
2-Methyl napthalene	70	670
Napthalene	160	2,100
Phenanthrene	240	1,500
Benz(a)anthracene	261	1,600
Benzo(a)pyrene	430	1,600
Chrysene	384	2,800
Dibenzo(a,h)anthracene	63.4	260
Fluoranthene	600	5,100
Pyrene	665	2,600
Low molecular weight PAH	552	3,160
High molecular weight PAH	1,700	9,600
Total PAHs	4,020	44,800
4,4'-DDE	2.2	27
Total DDT	1.6	46.1
Total PCBs	22.7	180

[a] Units are ug/g dry sediment, equivalent to ppm.
[b] Units are ng/g dry sediment, equivalent to ppb.

Sediment contaminant availability or organic enrichment can be altered in areas where there is considerable deposition of organic matter. Sediment toxicity from organic matter is assessed by measuring TOC. The criteria for rating TOC for individual sampling sites are shown in Table 4.

After sediment contaminants, and sediment TOC were assessed for a given site, the sediment quality index rating was calculated for the site and park based on these three indicators. The sediment quality index was rated good to poor for each site using the criteria shown in Table 4.

Table 4.
Condition criteria for sediment chemistry measures.

Rating	Sediment Contaminants Rating (SC)	% Total Organic Carbon (TOC)	Site Sediment Quality Index (SQI)	Park Sediment Quality Index
Good	No ERM concentrations are exceeded and less than five ERL concentrations are exceeded.	< 2%	TOC is good and Sediment Contaminants Rating is good.	Less than 5% of the sites are rated in *Poor* condition and less than 50% of the sites are rated in combined *Poor* and *Fair* condition.
Fair	Five or more ERL concentrations are exceeded.	2% – 5%	TOC is fair or Sediment Contaminants Rating is fair.	5% to 15% of sites are in *Poor* condition, or more than 50% of sites are in combined *Poor* and *Fair* condition.
Poor	An ERM concentration is exceeded for one or more contaminants	> 5%	TOC is poor or Sediment Contaminants Indicator is poor.	More than 15% of sites are in *Poor* condition

Summary Assessments

Figures 4 through 10 display the summary assessments for each water quality and sediment parameter measured.

Water Chemistry

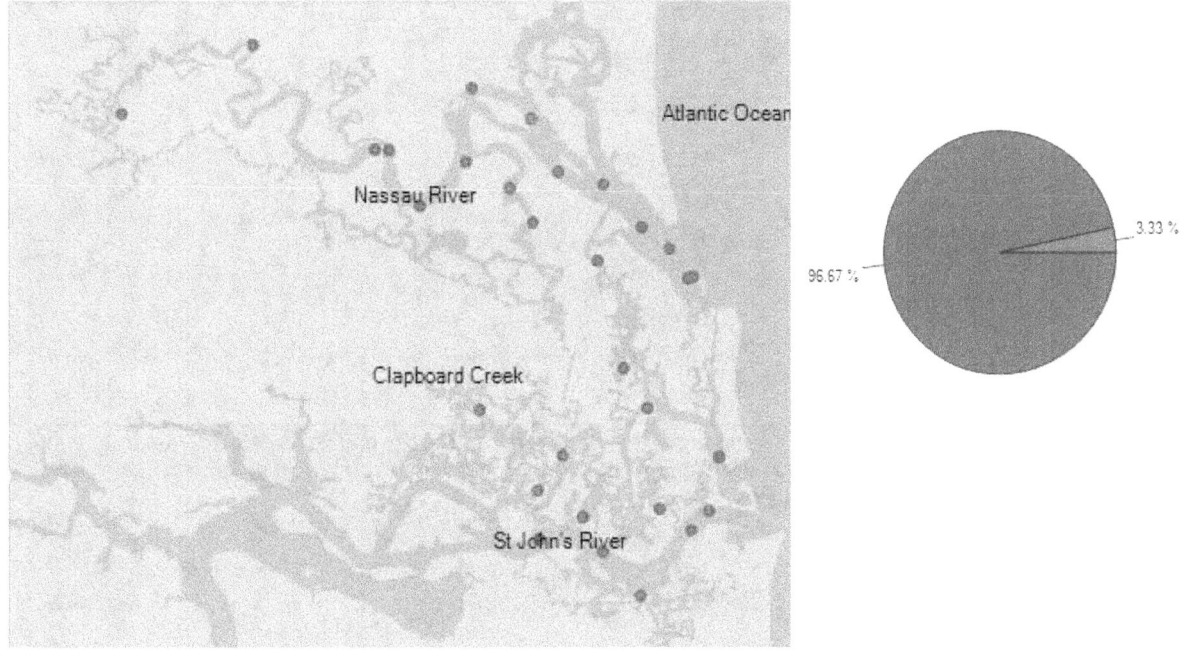

Figure 4. Assessment of Water Clarity Index scores at Timucuan Ecological and Historic Preserve, 2008, and percentage of sites in each condition category. Sites denoted as green received a *Good* rating, yellow sites ranked *Fair*, and red sites ranked *Poor*.

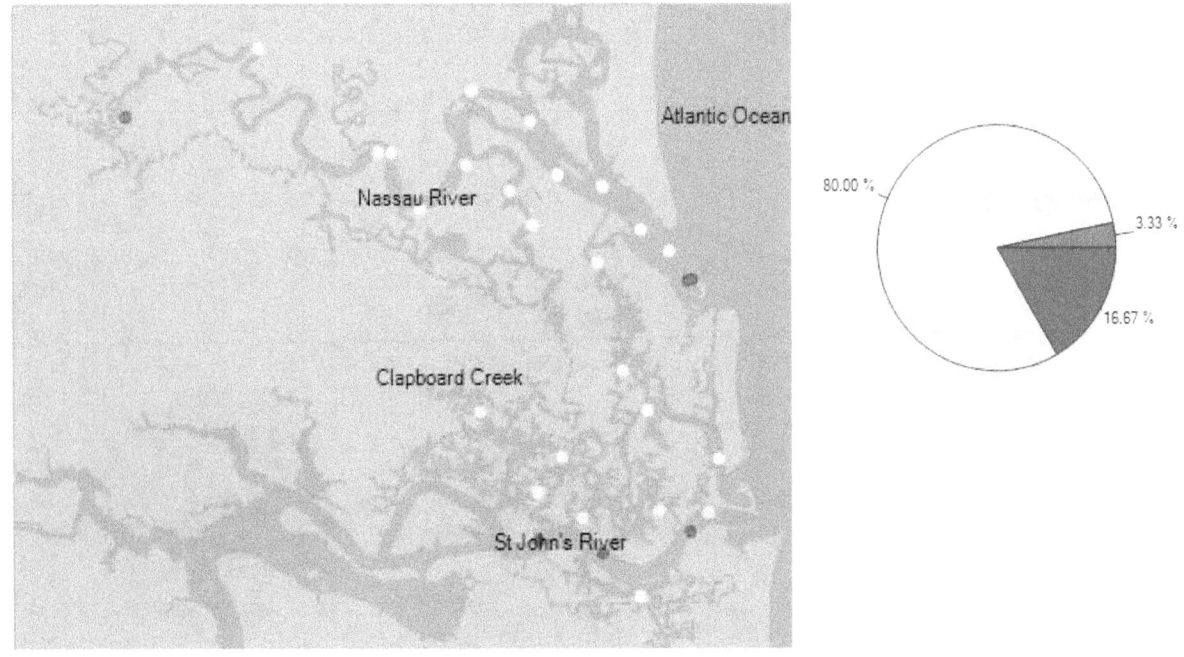

Figure 5. Assessment of Chlorophyll a concentrations at Timucuan Ecological and Historic Preserve, 2008, and percentage of sites in each condition category. Sites denoted as green received a *Good* rating, yellow sites ranked *Fair*, and red sites ranked *Poor*.

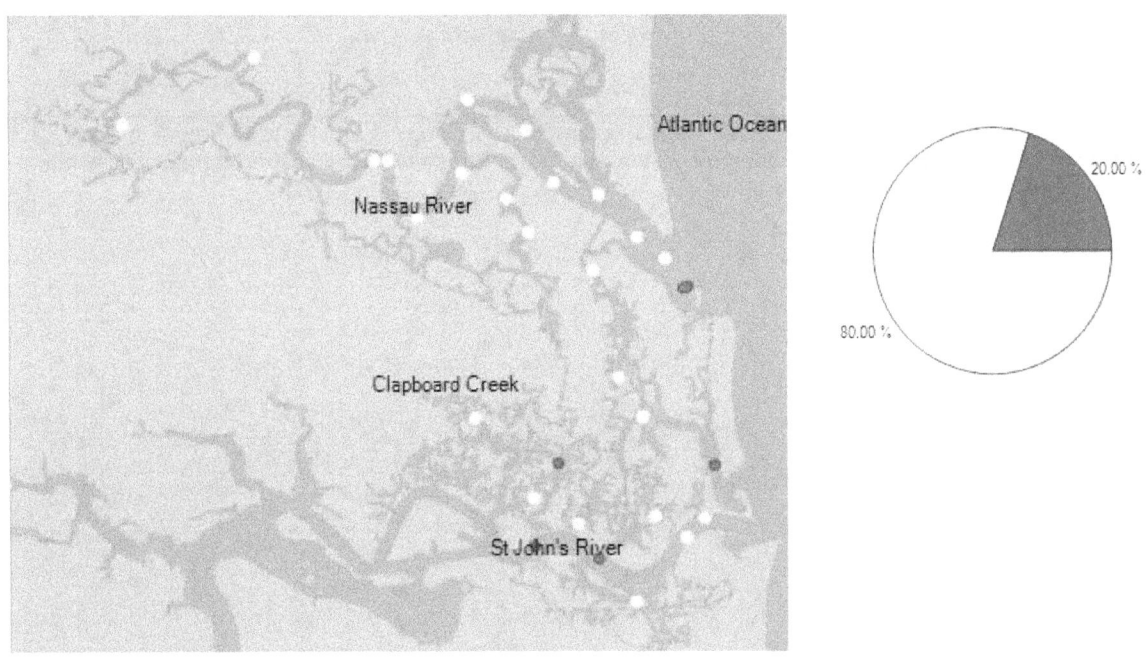

Figure 6. Assessment of Total Dissolved Nitrogen concentrations at Timucuan Ecological and Historic Preserve, 2008, and percentage of sites in each condition category. Sites denoted as green received a *Good* rating, yellow sites ranked *Fair*, and red sites ranked *Poor*.

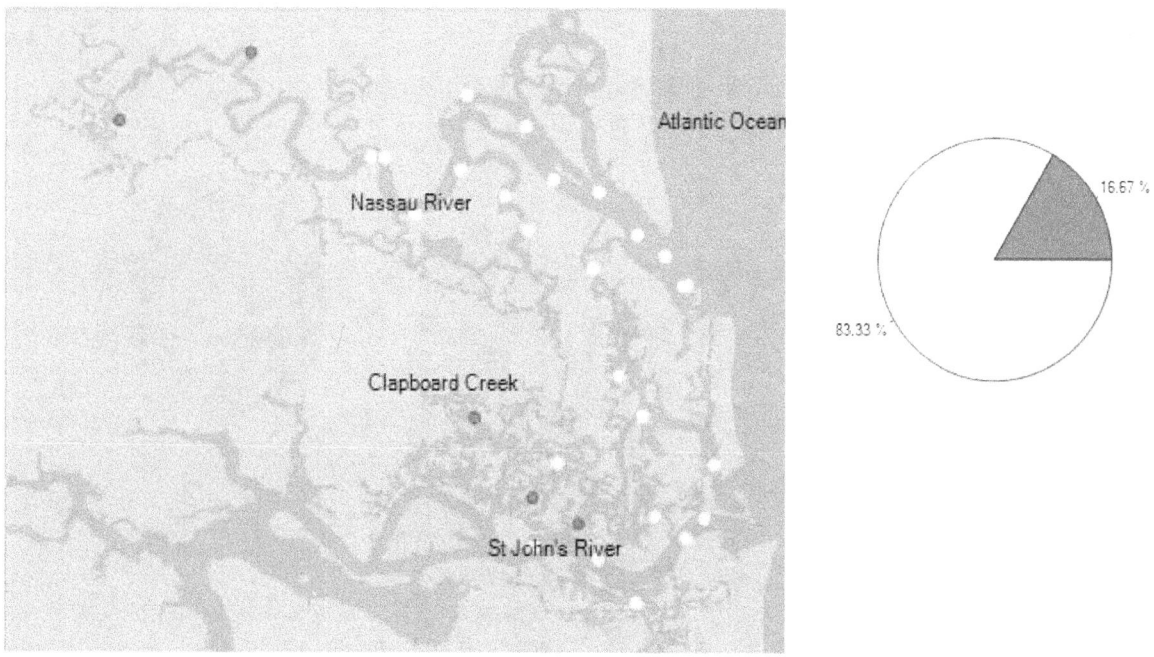

Figure 7. Assessment of Total Dissolved Phosphorus concentrations at Timucuan Ecological and Historic Preserve, 2008, and percentage of sites in each condition category. Sites denoted as green received a *Good* rating, yellow sites ranked *Fair*, and red sites ranked *Poor*.

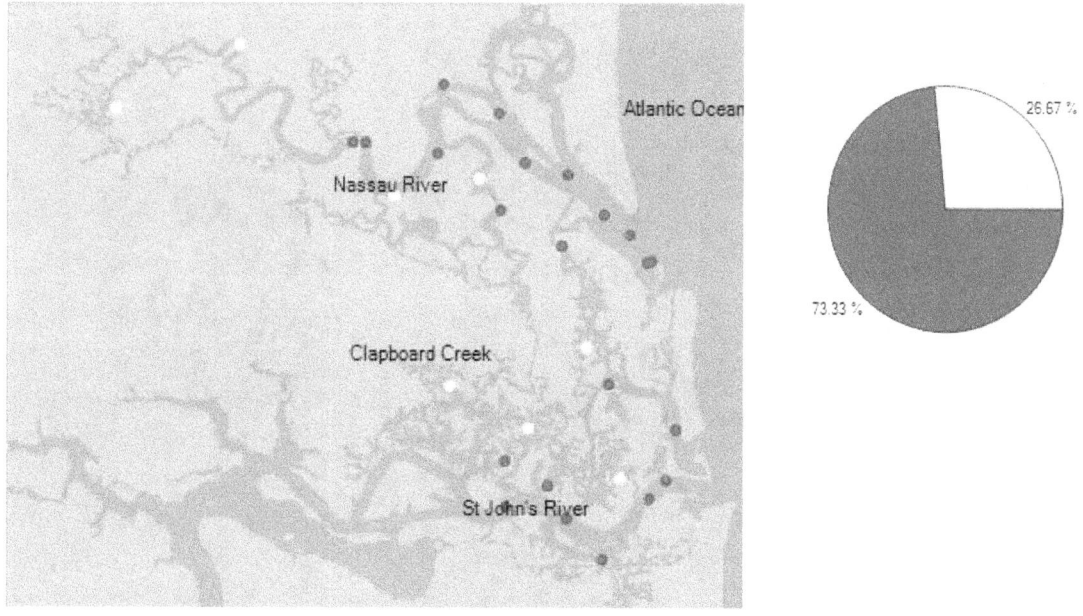

Figure 8. Assessment of Dissolved Oxygen concentrations at Timucuan Ecological and Historic Preserve, 2008, and percentage of sites in each condition category. Sites denoted as green received a *Good* rating, yellow sites ranked *Fair*, and red sites ranked *Poor*.

Sediment Chemistry

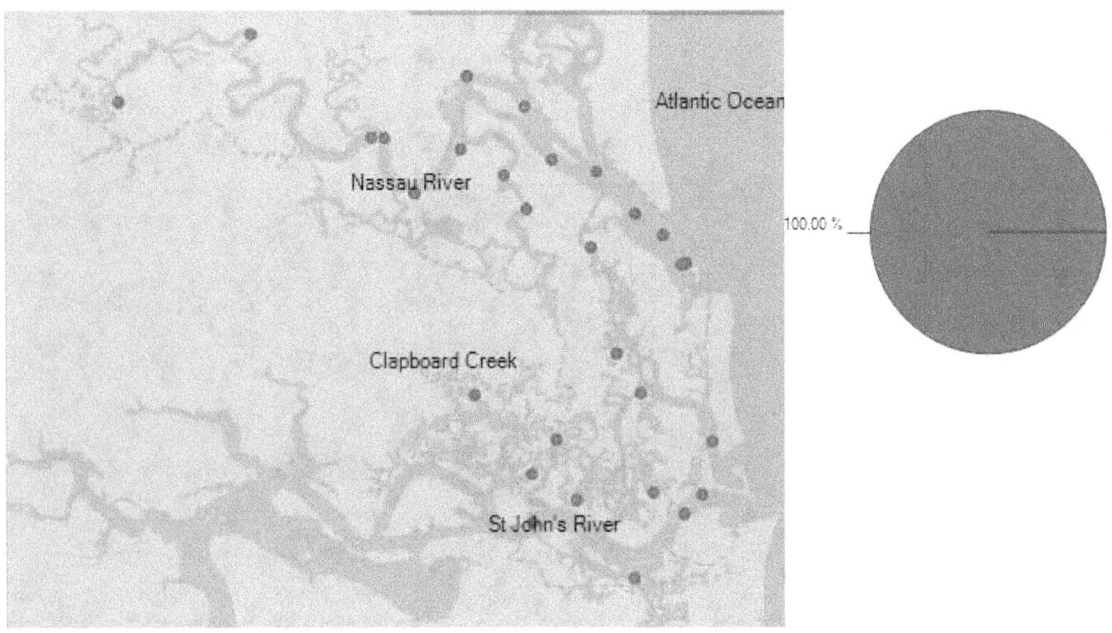

Figure 9. Assessment of Sediment Contaminants Index at Timucuan Ecological and Historic Preserve, 2008, and percentage of sites in each condition category. Sites denoted as green received a *Good* rating, yellow sites ranked *Fair*, and red sites ranked *Poor*.

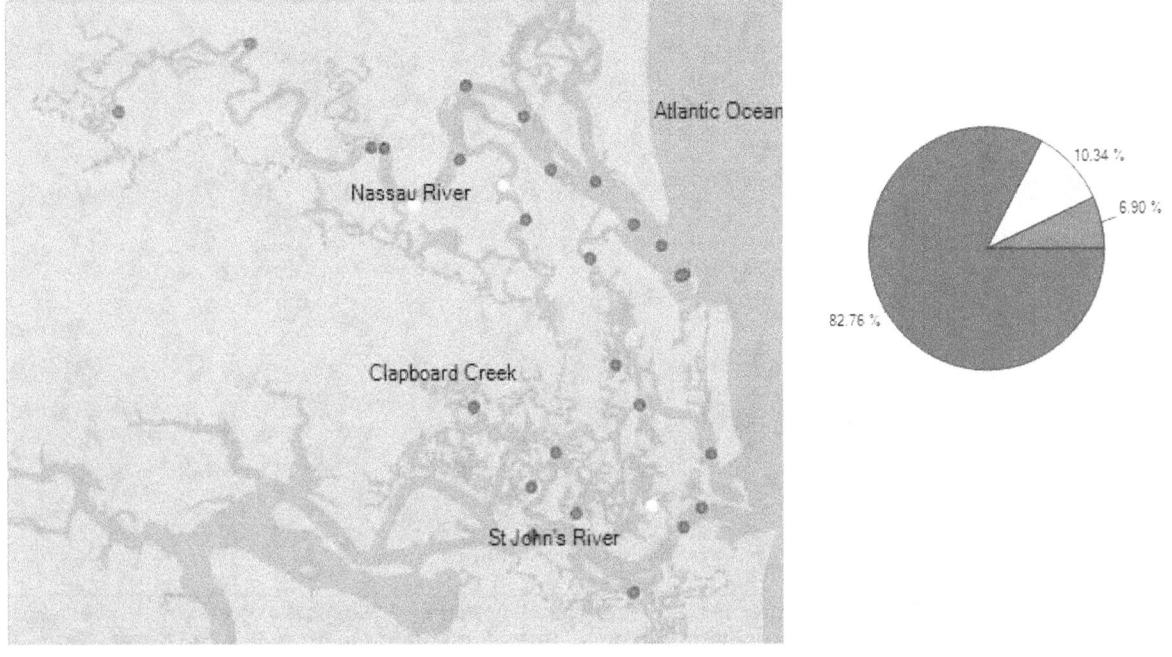

Figure 10. Assessment of Total Organic Carbon concentrations in sediments at Timucuan Ecological and Historic Preserve, 2008, and percentage of sites in each condition category. Sites denoted as green received a *Good* rating, yellow sites ranked *Fair*, and red sites ranked *Poor*.

Data

Water Chemistry

Table 5.
Water quality data for sites sampled at Timucuan Ecological and Historic Preserve, July 2009. Green values ranked as "Good," yellow sites ranked "Fair," and red sites ranked "Poor."

Station	Water Clarity Index (WCI)	Chlorophyl a (ug/L)	Total Dissolved Nitrogen (mg/L)	Total Dissolved Phosphorus (mg/L)	Dissolved Oxygen (mg/L)
TIMU-21	0.838	6.620	0.113	0.033	5.690
TIMU-12	0.850	9.745	0.155	0.032	5.330
TIMU-02	1.022	8.914	0.110	0.028	5.950
TIMU-18	2.000	2.118	0.092	0.023	6.920
TIMU-25	2.000	2.476	0.081	0.023	6.940
TIMU-06	2.000	8.722	0.102	0.026	7.010
TIMU-24	0.462	10.429	0.140	0.033	6.030
TIMU-20	0.626	13.183	0.126	0.034	5.300
TIMU-16	2.000	27.583	0.263	0.077	4.830
TIMU-28	0.850	16.793	0.305	0.061	4.660
TIMU-15	0.427	12.672	0.171	0.044	5.370
TIMU-27	0.626	13.596	0.147	0.043	5.040
TIMU-10	2.000	12.842	0.214	0.046	4.860
TIMU-08	0.850	6.125	0.199	0.048	5.010
TIMU-04	1.022	7.372	0.214	0.049	4.770
TIMU-09	1.222	17.550	0.255	0.041	5.460
TIMU-ALT-01	1.500	5.458	0.131	0.044	5.110
TIMU-14	1.222	5.516	0.133	0.041	4.910
TIMU-03	0.629	3.311	0.086	0.031	5.780
TIMU-07	0.397	3.070	0.069	0.037	5.780
TIMU-23	0.850	8.039	0.154	0.053	5.010
TIMU-01	0.715	4.450	0.177	0.038	5.600
TIMU-05	0.463	5.170	0.128	0.046	5.970
TIMU-13	1.500	6.489	0.175	0.066	4.440
TIMU-11	1.500	6.523	0.095	0.047	4.330
TIMU-29	2.000	6.452	0.072	0.026	5.690
TIMU-19	1.500	8.542	0.179	0.060	5.420
TIMU-17	1.042	8.410	0.139	0.045	4.420
TIMU-ALT-03	1.022	8.828	0.114	0.036	5.870
TIMU-ALT-02	5.000	8.594	0.192	0.033	5.410

Sediment Chemistry

Table 6.
Metals concentrations (in ppm) for sites sampled at Timucuan Ecological and Historic Preserve, July, 2008. Green values ranked as "Good," yellow sites ranked "Fair," and red sites ranked "Poor." Blue indicates missing / unavailable data.

Station	Arsenic	Cadmium	Chromium	Copper	Lead	Mercury	Nickel	Silver	Zinc
TIMU-01	4.6	0.26	9.7	7.4	11.9	0.016	4.8	0.49	21.5
TIMU-02	4	0.26	1.6	1.4	3.2	0.0063	1.3	0.49	17.7
TIMU-04	0.18	0.0051	47.9	0.2	0.36	0.042	0.32	0.0097	1
TIMU-05	3.9	0.25	0.8	1.6	5.6	0.0063	1.7	0.48	7.8
TIMU-06	3.9	0.25	1.6	0.81	1.7	0.0063	1.2	0.48	2.1
TIMU-07	4.1	0.25	3.2	4.4	9	0.0063	2.6	0.48	13.3
TIMU-08	3.9	0.25	1.6	1.3	3.3	0.0063	1.2	0.48	3.6
TIMU-09	4	0.26	0.8	3.3	6.9	0.011	5.1	0.49	15.7
TIMU-10	12.55	0.255	55.45	7	15.85	0.0175	14.25	0.485	43.15
TIMU-11	5.95	0.385	1.2	2	6.3	0.0094	2.95	0.73	15.7
TIMU-12	4	0.26	1.6	0.96	2	0.0063	1.3	0.49	12.9
TIMU-13	4	0.26	0.8	2	3.9	0.0063	1.3	0.49	5.9
TIMU-14	6.7	0.25	10.7	12.8	21.1	0.023	10.9	0.48	55.5
TIMU-15	3.9	2.2	1.6	4.2	5.4	0.0063	5.8	2.7	18.1
TIMU-16	8.5	2.8	29.2	8.2	18.4	0.043	14.7	2.9	48.7
TIMU-17		0.25	5.4	4.4	10.1	0.021	5.5	0.48	21.1
TIMU-18	3.95	0.255	1.6	0.935	2.9	0.0063	1.25	0.485	11.5
TIMU-19		0.25	7.3	6.2	14.1	0.016	4.8	0.48	28
TIMU-20	4.4	2.3	1.6	4.9	9.9	0.0063	7.2	2.8	22.6
TIMU-21	3.9	0.25	1.6	3.1	6.6	0.0063	2.2	0.48	18
TIMU-23	4	0.26	0.8	2.8	5.6	0.0063	2	0.49	14
TIMU-24	3.9	0.25	1.6	1.1	1.9	0.0063	1.2	0.48	4.2
TIMU-25	4	0.26	1.6	0.78	2.6	0.0063	1.3	0.49	13.7
TIMU-27	3.9	2.6	1.6	4.1	4.9	0.0063	5.6	2.8	19.1
TIMU-28	9.2	2.4	29.7	9.1	21.1	0.046	16.1	2.9	52.4
TIMU-29		0.25	0.79	1.4	4.7	0.0062	1.3	0.48	4.2
TIMU-ALT-01	3.9	0.25	13.3	5	7.3	0.018	3.4	0.48	19.4
TIMU-ALT-02		0.26	0.81	2.8	10.2	0.0063	3.5	0.49	13.3
TIMU-ALT-03		0.25	0.8	0.75	2.5	0.019	1.2	0.48	2

Table 7.
Organic contaminant concentrations (in ppm) for sites sampled at Timucuan Ecological and Historic Preserve, July, 2008. Green values ranked as "Good," yellow sites ranked "Fair," and red sites ranked "Poor." Blue sites contained missing data.

Station	2-Methylnaphthalene	4,4-DDE	Acenaphthene	Acenaphthylene	Anthracene	Benzo(a)anthracene	Benzo(a)pyrene	Chrysene	Dibenz(a,h)Anthracene	Fluoranthene	Fluorene	Naphthalene	Phenanthrene	Pyrene	Total DDT	High molecular weight PAH	Low molecular weight PAH	Total PAHs	Total PCBs
TIMU-01	5	0.5	5	5	0.99	4.2	0.99	3.2	5	5	5	5	1.7	3.7	1	40.77	58.43	99.2	21
TIMU-02	1	0.5	10	10	10	10	10	10	10	10	10	1	1	10	1	120	113	233	21
TIMU-04	1.9	0.5	1.9	1.9	1.9	1.9	1.9	1.9	1.9	1.9	1.9	1.9	1.9	1.9	1	22.8	26.6	49.4	21
TIMU-05	5.3	0.5	5.3	5.3	5.3	5.3	5.3	5.3	5.3	5.3	5.3	5.3	5.3	5.3	1	63.6	74.2	137.8	21
TIMU-06	10	0.5	10	10	10	10	10	10	10	10	10	10	10	10	1	120	140	260	21
TIMU-07	5.6	0.5	5.6	5.6	0.56	2.2	1.4	3.1	5.6	3.1	5.6	5.6	1.7	3.4	1	45.1	69.46	114.56	21
TIMU-08	6.3	0.5	6.3	6.3	6.3	6.3	6.3	6.3	6.3	6.3	6.3	6.3	6.3	6.3	1	75.6	88.2	163.8	21
TIMU-09	4.1	0.5	4.1	4.1	4.1	4.1	4.1	4.1	4.1	4.1	4.1	4.1	4.1	4.1	1	49.2	57.4	106.6	21
TIMU-10	3	0.5	3	3	3	3	3	3	3	3	3	3	3	3	1	36	42	78	21
TIMU-11	5.6	0.5	5.6	5.6	5.6	5.6	5.6	5.6	5.6	5.6	5.6	5.6	5.6	3.35	1	64.95	78.4	143.35	21
TIMU-12	2	0.5	10	1.5	1.5	2.5	2	2.5	10	2.5	1.5	2	2	2	1	50.5	30	80.5	21
TIMU-13	6	0.5	6	6	6	6	6	6	6	6	6	6	6	6	1	72	84	156	21
TIMU-14	3.1	0.5	3.1	3.1	3.1	1.2	0.78	1.1	3.1	2.3	3.1	3.1	1.1	1.9	1	22.32	41.4	63.72	21
TIMU-15	10	0.5	10	10	10	10	10	10	10	10	10	1	10	10	1	120	131	251	21
TIMU-16	1	0.5	10	10	10	10	10	10	10	10	10	1	10	10	1	120	122	242	21
TIMU-17	10	0.5	10	10	10	10	10	10	10	10	10	10	10	10	1	120	140	260	20.92
TIMU-18	1	0.5	6.25	10	10	27	10	34.5	10	42	12	1	5.5	22	2.55	201.75	115.75	317.5	21.8
TIMU-19	10	0.5	10	10	10	2.5	1.5	3	10	5.5	10	10	2	5.5	1	73.5	132	205.5	21
TIMU-20	1	0.5	10	10	10	10	10	10	10	10	10	1	1	10	1	120	113	233	21
TIMU-21	10	0.5	10	10	10	10	10	10	10	10	10	10	10	10	1	120	140	260	21
TIMU-23	5.9	0.5	5.9	5.9	5.9	5.9	5.9	5.9	5.9	1.5	5.9	5.9	5.9	1.5	1	62	82.6	144.6	21
TIMU-24	1	0.5	10	10	10	10	10	10	10	10	10	1	10	10	1	120	122	242	21
TIMU-25	10	0.5	10	10	10	10	10	10	10	1	10	1	10	10	1	111	131	242	21
TIMU-27	10	0.5	10	10	10	10	10	10	10	10	10	10	10	10	3.5	120	140	260	21
TIMU-28	1	0.5	10	10	10	10	10	1.5	10	2	10	1	1	10	1	103.5	113	216.5	21
TIMU-29	10	0.5	10	10	10	10	10	10	10	10	10	10	10	10	1	120	140	260	21
TIMU-ALT-01	6	0.5	6	6	6	6	6	6	6	1.5	6	6	0.9	1.2	1	62.7	78.9	141.6	21
TIMU-ALT-02	10	0.5	10	10	10	10	10	10	10	10	10	10	10	10	1	120	140	260	21
TIMU-ALT-03	10	0.5	10	10	10	10	10	10	10	10	10	10	10	10	1	120	140	260	21

Table 8.
Sediment contaminants rating (SC), percent total organic carbon (TOC), and Sediment Quality Index (SQI) rating for sites sampled at Timucuan Ecological and Historic Preserve, July, 2008. Green values ranked as "Good," yellow sites ranked "Fair," and red sites ranked "Poor."

Station	SC	TOC	SQI
TIMU-01	Good	1.4	Good
TIMU-02	Good	0.32	Good
TIMU-04	Good	5	Fair
TIMU-05	Good	0.49	Good
TIMU-06	Good	0.41	Good
TIMU-07	Good	1.2	Good
TIMU-08	Good	0.36	Good
TIMU-09	Good	1.6	Good
TIMU-10	Good	4.05	Fair
TIMU-11	Good	1.31	Good
TIMU-12	Good	0.42	Good
TIMU-13	Good	0.64	Good
TIMU-14	Good	2.8	Fair
TIMU-15	Good	0.59	Good
TIMU-16	Good	5.6	Poor
TIMU-17	Good	1.4	Good
TIMU-18	Good	0.285	Good
TIMU-19	Good	0.91	Good
TIMU-20	Good	0.98	Good
TIMU-21	Good	0.6	Good
TIMU-23	Good	0.63	Good
TIMU-24	Good	0.29	Good
TIMU-25	Good	0.28	Good
TIMU-27	Good	0.74	Good
TIMU-28	Good	5.7	Poor
TIMU-29	Good	0.7	Good
TIMU-ALT-01	Good	0.41	Good
TIMU-ALT-02	Good	1.2	Good
TIMU-ALT-03	Good	0.3	Good

Literature Cited

DeVivo, J. C., C. J. Wright, M. W. Byrne, E. DiDonato, and T. Curtis. 2008. Vital signs monitoring in the Southeast Coast Inventory & Monitoring Network. Natural Resource Report NPS/SECN/NRR—2008/061. National Park Service, Fort Collins, Colorado.

Holland, A. F., D. M. Sanger, C. P. Gawle, S. B. Lerberg, M. S. Santiago, G. H. M. Riekerk, L. E. Zimmerman, and G. I. Scott. 2004. Linkages between tidal creek ecosystems and the landscape and demographic attributes of their wetlands. Journal of Experimental Marine Biology and Ecology 298:151-178.

Lerberg, S. B., A. F. Holland, and D. Sanger. 2000. Responses of tidal creek macrobenthic communities to the effects of watershed development. Estuaries 23(6):838-853.

Long, E. R., D. D. MacDonald, S. L. Smith, and F. D. Calder. 1995. Incidence of adverse biological effects within ranges of chemical concentrations in marine and estuarine sediments. Environmental Management 19(1):81–97.

Stevens, D. L., Jr. 1997. Variable density grid-based sampling designs for continuous spatial populations. Environmentric 8:167-195.

Stevens, D. L., Jr. and Olsen, A.R. 1999. Spatially restricted surveys over time for aquatic resources. Journal of Agricu ltural, Biological and Environmental Statistics 4:415-428.

Stevens, D. and A. R. Olsen. 2004. Spatially balanced sampling of natural resources. Journal of the American Statistical Association 99:262-278.

U.S. EPA. 2001. Environmental Monitoring an Assessment Program (EMAP). National Coastal Assessment Quality Assurance Project Plan 2001 – 2004. United States Environmental Protection Agency, Office of Research and Development, National Health and Environmental Effects Research Laboratory, gulf Ecology Division, gulf Breeze, FL. EPA/620/R-01/002.

U.S. EPA. 2005. National Coastal Condition Report II. EPA-620/R-03/002. Office of Research and Development and Office of Water, Washington, D.C., USA.

NPS 100008, May 2009